LOVE LETTERS:
THE TIMELESS TREASURE

Ann Marie Ruby

Disclaimer:
This book ("*Love Letters: The Timeless Treasure*") does not represent
or endorse any religious, philosophical, political or scientific view. This
book has been written in good faith for people of all cultures and
beliefs.

Published in the United States of America, 2020.

ISBN-10: 0-578-82455-8

ISBN-13: 978-0-578-82455-0

DEDICATION

"Like the phoenix, from ashes we arose. For you my love, eternally I am, as for me eternally you are. In union, we are one."

-Ann Marie Ruby

Twin flames are two yet one. They awaken throughout time for one another. A poem written in the name of a beloved unites two souls into one through words. A vow taken by two in front of God, becomes a poem through words.

In honor of all twin flames crossing time and tide to be one throughout eternity, I have written this book of poetry. I dedicate this book to my twin flame who had appeared within my dreams. For thousands of nights, I have waited for you. I know we will find one another one day. Yet today, I have written these poems which are sweet songs from my heart, sung with all my love, for you.

May all my love be with you.

MESSAGE FROM THE AUTHOR

"Thousands of years of waiting, became a day as I had my poems of love create a bridge to unite you and me throughout time."

-Ann Marie Ruby

Throughout time, love has united us with one another. Love stories come upon our hands when they end in grief, yet I believe love wins either way. Waiting for someone special for even thousands of years is worth the wait.

Love does not end in death as this blessed oath lives across time. Through memories created for one another, this bond crosses all time. You must believe in the magical spell of this enchantment for then you too will enter the mesmerized world of eternal love.

Today, travel with me through some love letters. In a poetic way, I have written them for you to cherish and keep eternally. These poems will take you on a journey where love is always victorious.

Within these poems, I have crossed all borders to bind my charmed love letters in a book. These poems are for all of whom have dreamt of falling in love. Read them and know if you have not found him or her, there is always hope. If you have a special person in your life, then read with that person and fall in love again.

Pass these poems to your children and grandchildren. Send them a handwritten note saying love is within your inner soul. Believe in this magical spell for the enchanting land of love is only an imagination and a poem away.

Life will be a blessing the day you finally believe in true love. I believe in twin flames and their journey. My poems are my blessings and prayers sent your way. These poems are gifted with a complete imagery created for the individual poem as an individual story on her own. Cherish each poem completely as you can walk within each illustration and be a part of the etenal love story created just for you.

I had asked myself a thousand times, how are the stories in my poems different from the real-life true stories. The answer is they are all the same, yet I painted them differently within my art of poems. For they are all my "what if I had you." The difference between a poet and a scientist is simple. I see the skies kiss the Earth. The sun comes down to Earth from the skies and blesses both with his ray and glow. The grass is made out of rainbows and love.

The scientists will tell you the skies never touch the Earth, the sun never comes down to the Earth, and the grass is not made out of rainbows or love. I would actually ask, "Really?" Yet both are correct as that's why one is a scientist, and the other is a poet with a pen and paper where she writes "what if."

In this book, however, I have done a lot of research to keep scientific facts alive, such as the birds which sing for us throughout the night, moonbows and rainbows, and much more. This is my book of poetry where "what if" comes into play, which includes the inner love, imagery, and a lot of my enchanted and magical art. This book also is the enchanted spells of, only if you were mine.

If you were mine, I would paint the skies and Earth as kissing one another. There would be clouds sitting on top of the sea, and on top of the cloud would be my beloved holding me within his embrace. Yes, this poetry book is the enchanted love of, only if you were mine.

I hope and pray all the hands that touch these poems, find their other half through this book of poetry. May this book be your tranquility and peace as you take a journey through the magical land of love. Do enjoy my book of poetry. Cherish true love and may my *Love Letters: The Timeless Treasure* be there for you and your twin flame throughout time.

TABLE OF CONTENTS

INTRODUCTION

"Love is an eternal treasure land, where lovers create poems through magical words, originating from one soul to the other."

-Ann Marie Ruby

There is no sight of beginning nor is there any sight of ending, for love is eternal. Within the lovers' lane, forever yours my love, is and shall always be a promise eternally recited and kept by the eternal lovers. Today for you and your forever love, I have my book of eternal love poems. Throughout time, we have found lovebirds flying together, singing in tune with one another. Today with this book in your hands, you too can recite these enchanted love poems.

The human lovebirds throughout the night skies and throughout time, have sought one another. They find the eternal comfort of being complete only when united with one another. This holy union was, is, and shall always be everlasting. Even when all is lost and nothing is found, the poems of true lovers and their personal love songs shall live on. The enchanted love poems from this book can be heard throughout time, even when the lovers cannot be heard anymore.

We the human population have found upon our hands, love stories that have crossed time and space. Love stories have crossed race, color, and religion. Love stories have crossed the realm of mortality and have come back as memories making themselves eternal. I bring to you my book of love poems, honoring the endless love stories of twin flames.

This book has been created through the spiritual inspiration found within eternal twin flames. I realized this life leaves behind for all of us the greatest gift any human could ever ask for or about. This sacred blessed gift is known to you and me as the gift of love.

Love is eternal, for no signed paper or documentation is needed to seal this blessing. Love seals forever two souls in an eternal bond throughout time. Time leaves us at the end of her journey, yet through love even time freezes. As love becomes eternal, everything around her too becomes eternal.

Eternity finds life through love. Love is blessed through true lovers. For this sanctified reason, to honor all sacred lovers throughout time, and their timeless journey through love, I have named my book of romantic poetry,

Love Letters: The Timeless Treasure.

BE MY LIFELINE

Stranded, lost, and lonely,

I strolled on my own.

Yet I was never lonely or lost

For throughout time,

You held on to me.

My breathing was never mine

As your breathing was never yours.

My heartbeats were loud and clear in your chest,

As your heartbeats I felt within my chest.

Never feared the fearful

As I held on to your hands.

Your hands held on to me

Even throughout the roughest rides.

I felt sheltered within your chest.

Promises we made,

Promises we shall keep,

Life after life.

Oh my love, my beloved,

Even throughout time,

I shall be yours,

As you are and shall eternally,

BE MY LIFELINE.

BEYOND BORDERS

Moon shines her true grandeur,

Upon the thriving waters

Of the sea.

Wind chimes dance within the ears of all on

Land, sea, and air.

The seawater splashes upon land

As they kiss and dance with joy.

Love is created from far beyond,

As she spreads upon the Earth.

Life is a song bursting with love,

As you hold on to me.

Dancing under the skies,

We keep the stars as our observers.

The roaring sea starts singing,

With high waves for she too

Wants to be a part of this story.

The wind plays musical flutes

Of harmony,

For he too wants to be a part of this unification.

The moon above the skies,

Flickers to shine like a lantern,

As she too wants to be a part of this blessed union.

Mother Earth smiles as she becomes a watcher.

For all her children in the present and future,

She sings the sweet songs of our love story,

Throughout time for all,

BEYOND BORDERS.

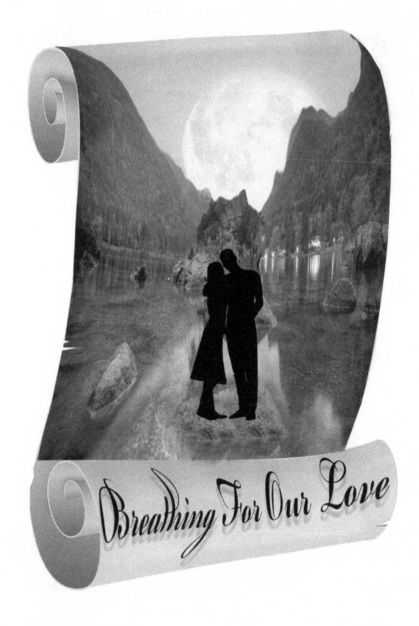

BREATHING
FOR OUR LOVE

Love is born through God's grace.

For you,

I was created,

As you were created

For only me.

My heart started singing

As she found you.

Throughout time, I sought you,

Yet I found you as you found me.

My heart felt your heartbeats,

And jolted back to life.

Apart from you,

I am alive,

Yet my heart feels incomplete.

United with you, I am complete.

My existence on Earth found a reason,

As you appeared within my life.

Your devoutness toward our union,

Your emergence calls for our love,

United twin flames.

Forever, eternally sanctified,

This twin flame is

BREATHING

FOR OUR LOVE.

BURNING HEARTS

Sun's rays heat up the seawater,

Yet there is no fire.

The warmth and comfort

Spread through the lands,

As this heat finds a home

Within the inner souls of all lovers.

You and I too are blessed by this love,

As we walk hand in hand,

Upon the warm seashore.

We leave behind

Our footprints on the sand.

The lovers' print we create,

Is a heart with Cupid's arrow.

Becoming an ark,

She floats from sea to the lands,

Crossing time and tide.

Never is she washed away,

Never is she erased,

And never is she in danger of elimination,

For she is the eternal burning desire of love,

Created by the eternal lovers of

BURNING HEARTS.

Candle And Flame

CANDLE
AND FLAME

Rising from ashes,

We have taken rebirth.

You became the river,

I became your waterfall.

Everywhere you are,

I am found.

So, from your feelings,

I am felt.

For wherever you go,

I shall always follow.

Separated we are to be an individual,

Yet united we are as one.

Within your heartbeats,

I am complete.

Inside my heartbeats,

You are complete.

In union,

We become the eternal twin flames,

For you are the passion I burn within,

For in union,

We are,

CANDLE

AND FLAME.

DEPTH OF MY EYES

Eyes are our observers,

Life after life.

You had asked me to let you see me

For one more minute.

Nights sailed by and days flourished by,

Yet we only knew one another.

Within your eyes, I found the remedies

For my unsought questions.

As we gazed upon one another,

We saw the universe in front of us.

The astounding night stars I found in front of me.

I ascended upon the mountain top,

Just by sitting there with you.

I had seen your tenderness for me,

As you saw my tenderness for you,

Just by watching within our united souls.

For my love, this twin flame needs nothing,

Be it physical,

Or be it spiritual.

My mind, body, and soul only need you.

My dear guarded me as he replied,

All the questions,

And answers of my life,

Were fully visible,

Within the

DEPTH OF MY EYES.

DESTINY

Ordained to one another,

Throughout all the darkness and light.

Fate plays a mesmerizing flute,

Intoxicating all through sounds of musical tunes.

I waited for fate

To knock upon my door.

The ever-so-prevailing destiny

Will come at his will.

Tears rolled down as I told fate,

I was not ready for him.

I had so many unwritten love letters

I must send to my beloved.

I asked fate what he had in store for me tonight.

A spellbinding romantic night,

Was very secluded.

Neither did the night know what was in her future,

Nor did she preplan for it.

The night had found a confidante tonight,

A lonely traveler like myself.

I greeted the solitary stars.

One by one, they came.

Tonight, I forgot about fate and his plans.

It was then like a blazing light,

I found by my side,

Sitting under the same sky,

Gazing upon one another,

My beloved.

When I least anticipated,

Fate brought me the paramount gift

Of eternity,

My true soulmate, my twin flame.

It is then I appreciated,

Not to give up on fate,

For he finally unites us with our,

DESTINY.

DREAM

Tonight, the shimmering moon

Is shining upon the enchanted night skies.

All around, I see nightfall evolve.

My tired body wants to be aware of

What is to come,

Yet sleep takes over my physical body.

Bewitched scatterings of love

Fall upon my eyes.

I observed you appeared amid a mist.

I ran for you,

Only to realize you were a fantasy.

Then, I saw you again,

This time holding on to me.

Emotions split my soul,

As I slipped,

On the thorn-filled path of roses.

You placed your sweet kisses,

Upon my feet and removed all the thorns.

I knew the charming dust of magical love

Will escape my eyes,

With the first sight of dawn.

Yet I could not part myself from you.

So, I prayed

For you,

For me,

And for us.

I cried and asked you,

Not to part yourself from me.

May this blessed night

Never end.

Let these fragrances

From the enchanted

Spellbinding nights last

Forever,

Even if this is only my

DREAM.

Enchanted By Your Eyes

ENCHANTED
BY YOUR EYES

Alone and free

From the magical bewitchments of love, I was.

No fear of losing anyone or anything,

For I had nothing to gain or lose.

Like a fog of smoke, there you were,

Walking up from the dark seawater.

The stars were twinkling,

The moon was blushing.

I was lonely and free.

Nonetheless, I landed upon your path,

As you became my route.

I ran after you.

I wanted another glimpse of you

For I knew I had no other way to travel in life.

For me, there was only one approach,

Where my path and your path knotted

Through the pleasures of eternal love.

My feet halted in an instance.

My eyes froze in time.

Eternally, my mind, body, and soul remained,

ENCHANTED

BY YOUR EYES.

ETERNAL DESTINATION

Day develops with sunrise,

As she leaves us at sunset.

The trees bloom in spring,

Yet all the leaves fall during winter.

Destination for all actions

Is their reactions.

This lonesome heart answers to only you.

My oath of love is my action.

Lifelong celibacy until your coming is my wish,

For this soul only

Inclines toward you.

You are my only tug of life

For your words are music to my soul.

Your drives are my attraction of life.

Your breath is the stimulating air of nature.

Your heartbeats

Keep me alive.

Always through life,

Or even in death,

This twin flame shall descend only to you

For you are my

ETERNAL DESTINATION.

FLAMES OF DESIRE

Like phoenixes, we have flamed

And roused from ashes,

Retelling all it is time to be reborn again.

From ashes, we have risen,

To only find one another.

Twin flames we are,

As we have flamed up the night skies,

Seeking each other.

The burning flames keep us ablaze,

Yet this flame is only observable,

Through our eyes.

For this world,

Our flame is invisible as are we.

For you my love,

I keep the flame passionately,

Within my soul.

As I listen to your

Heartfelt musical tunes,

I ask you,

For me and only me,

Always keep safeguarded,

Your

FLAMES OF DESIRE.

FOR YOU, I AM

Enchanting night calls you,

The radiant moon of the night

Calls upon you,

For they are both apprehensive,

Where are you?

Mother Earth unearths you,

As she knows you are a traveler too.

You ask the entrancing nights,

The dazzling moon,

Mother Earth,

The same question,

Where am I?

Our search has created,

A storm upon the ravishing sea.

Like the rising phoenix,

We both discretely levitated from ashes,

Life after life,

Only to fuse with one another.

Our enchanted and spellbinding eternal love

Had woken Earth and Heaven above.

As all vibrated in harmony,

And knew,

We were created for one another,

Hence, we both sang in union,

FOR YOU, I AM.

FOREVER
YOU ARE MINE

Sweet temptation of the nightingale's

Musical voice pursues me.

My indulgent heart almost falls for the temptation,

Yet stops at the window

For I only seek you.

My kindred soul quests only your musical flute.

Life after life,

I waited at my window,

For your calls.

Nothing enticed my soul,

For I am your other half.

This mind, body, and soul shall awaken,

Only at your calls.

I close my windows,

To all nightingales pursuing one another.

Tonight is different.

The stars are all winking.

The moon is shining.

Mother Earth too,

Is singing with her children,

For all know,

Tonight,

My beloved has finally,

Arrived upon my shore.

Thousands of years,

I have waited for these nectar-filled,

Fragranced calls of my beloved.

Tonight,

After thousands of years of waiting,

Keeping Mother Nature as our witness,

You chanted,

FOREVER

YOU ARE MINE.

HEART BEAT ONLY MY NAME

Apart by land and sea,

By time and space,

Yet united through eternal bliss,

Between you and me.

Do you not reminisce our memories?

How you had held on to me?

How we were made for one another?

Remember my love, we had created eternal love stories,

Where the heavenly skies sent wishing stars.

Blue seawater danced with joy.

Mystical mountain breeze came down.

Mother Earth too joined in this with her musical guitars.

For you, I have initiated our union even before you came.

For eternally, I have prayed.

Forever I have wished, may my twin flame's

HEART BEAT ONLY MY NAME.

Heavenly Falls

HEAVENLY FALLS

Nature's musical recital,

Drummed on my roof.

My heavy eyes forced my

Stirred soul to stroll outside.

Tonight, Heaven and Earth were

Performing with joy.

Mother Nature was having a musical show,

Yet all lives were hiding in fear.

I did not fear,

For even on a stormy night,

My eyes sought one person.

I recited along with Mother Nature,

For I hoped she would somehow,

Send my love letters to my beloved.

The pouring skies

Would purify his feet.

The cool mountain breeze would

Comfort his soul.

The sound of nature's musical tunes

Would generate a musician in him.

I know it is time for him

To come to my door.

For how could he not come,

When Mother Nature has exhibited

For him a performance?

The night too knew,

My romantic heart,

Only desired my beloved.

So tonight,

They all called my beloved,

And revealed to him my door,

With the comfort of

HEAVENLY FALLS.

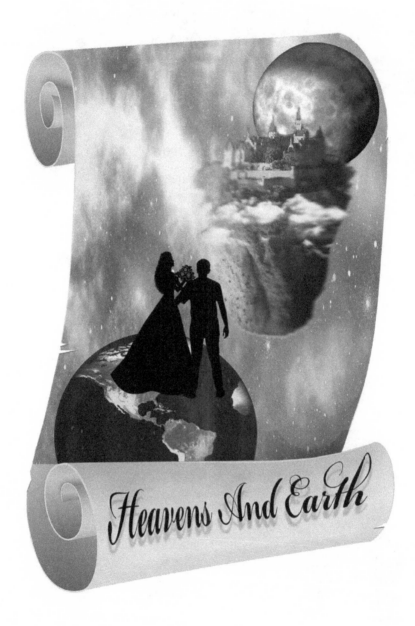

HEAVENS AND EARTH

Green grass flowers happily

All around the mountain.

Rivers whirl through

The green fields with love.

Mountains rise from Earth,

Hoping to reach the skies.

Mountain springs curve

Water into Earth as rain drizzles.

My heart and soul

Wish to be one like a raindrop in reversal,

Hence, I can flow back into your heart.

My love,

You are as big as the blissful skies,

And I am like the green Earth,

Then how do we unite?

We shall be like the droplets

Of rain and flow

From my heart to yours,

And from your heart to mine.
The pleasant water shall unite us,
Just as the sacred rain
Pouring upon Earth unites the
HEAVENS
AND EARTH.

I THEE WED

Lovers' rainbow appeared upon the blissful skies,

Chanting with this enchanted land.

Chiming windstorms came to town.

Today, my garden has flourished with

Eternal love.

My cottage has flowered

With daffodils, lilies, freesias, roses,

And wisterias.

The flower haven today has thrived for

True twin flames.

From ashes, we have risen like phoenixes,

Only to accept one another.

Thousands of years,

This dream garden,

Was asleep.

The snow-covered roses were all asleep.

Today, all of the flower pixies have returned.

Enchanted magical celebration

Is taking place today

For today my twin flame

Touched my lips.

This immortal kiss has

Awakened him and me.

Today, we the twin flames have united,

As we have taken the vows of

I THEE WED.

INFINITELY ELIMINATE
ALL HIS PAIN

Ocean's waves kissed my feet,

As I gifted her with my tears.

She sang her sweet songs to calm me down.

I still was unmoved by her words.

My feet were glued onto the white sandy strand,

As my inner soul only pursued him.

Within the ocean, I sought him.

Up above the skies, I gazed for him.

In the cold blowing breeze, I waited for him.

My tears flooded all around the white shore,

Yet I stayed positioned waiting only for him.

What if he comes and I miss him,

I thought.

What if he gets lost and needs my guidance,

I asked myself.

The water began to rise as I started to fall.

Abruptly, I was lifted from the flooding ocean water.

I saw my feet were not wet anymore,

Nor was I cold.

For now, I was within the embrace of warm cozy hands.

My love, my life had come,

When I was not watching.

I asked him when he came.

Why am I not drowning in the ocean water?

He answered,

Throughout time, eternally, he was there by my side,

Always waiting for me to realize,

As I am outrageously in love with him,

He too is eccentrically in love with me.

For his love for me,

And my love for him,

Throughout eternity, he never left.

He had taken all my pain upon himself,

So, I prayed,

Today, may my Lord

INFINITELY ELIMINATE

ALL HIS PAIN.

KEEPSAKE THROUGHOUT TIME

Memories molded with you.

Memories are complete for you.

In union,

We became a candle blushing in the dark.

Our candle glows

Within our love temple.

Your promise made to me

Sparks like a candle within my soul.

I have written our name with a burning candle,

In the temples of all lovers.

The path you have taken to voyage to me,

And I had taken to transport to you,

Has been given a name,

Entitled the lovers' lane.

This lane has been lit with glowing candles,

Which never fade nor burn out by the wind

For these candles are

Forever protected by

The loving hands of fortunate couples.

My love, my life,

I have made our love story,

The page of our life,

For all to have as a

KEEPSAKE

THROUGHOUT TIME.

Kisses From My Beloved

KISSES FROM MY BELOVED

Beds of flowers painted my path,

Mountain springs washed my hair,

As my beloved remained wide awake,

To shower me

With love.

Robins sat on my windowsill

Humming love songs all day.

Stars lit up the skies,

Illustrating a love heart

With Cupid's bow and arrow

As my darling had asked for it.

Morning glories,

Stimulate me

Each dawn with sweet fragrances

For my love makes it happen.

Tonight, I had asked,

The beds of flowers,

The mountain springs,

The robins,

The starlit skies,

And the intoxicating morning glories

To take a break.

As for tonight, tomorrow,

And for the rest of my life,

I don't need anything but

KISSES FROM MY BELOVED.

LOVE SURVIVES ALL

From ashes we rose,

Like the rising phoenix.

We crossed the ferrying gondolas,

And got on the Ferris wheel,

Only for one another,

Eternally trying to keep

The ribbon of love,

Tied on to one another.

Yet as we got stranded,

The night stars guided us.

The rising sun at dawn,

Gave us hope.

We sang the nightly songs,

To attract one another.

We appeared to one another,

Across time,

With the tied ribbon of faith.

We whirled across

Cold river lifelines,

Praying to keep

Our memories alive.

Finally, like a flying phoenix,

We flew into one another.

Nothing kept us apart.

As we befriended time and tide,

Flying and swimming against

All beliefs,

We landed at the door of love.

Keeping our love as witness,

We knew

All things shall end,

Except

LOVE SURVIVES ALL.

LOVERS' LAGOON

Fog covered night,

The moon is barely visible.

My love held on to me

As he said, even the moon is

Giving us privacy.

The night talked as we only

Talked with our eyes.

The gondolas ferrying lovebirds,

Passed by us.

Raindrops fell on top of us,

As my beloved told me,

They were our spilled tears,

For the time we were apart.

Nightingales started to sing,

Announcing it was the time

Of union

Between two souls,

Two flames,

Two individuals,

To be one.
This blessed merging
Of two souls
Shall be within the
LOVERS' LAGOON.

MIRROR IMAGE

Reflections within your eyes,

Stared back at my eyes.

I watched myself in your eyes.

All the thoughts I had,

Revitalized upon your eyes.

Nothing was said,

Nothing was asked,

Yet your smile answered all my questions.

All my solutions were written,

Upon your gazing stare.

Your encircled embrace warmed me

During times I felt cold.

Your sweet kisses disconnected all my fear.

Your hands grasped on to my hands

When I needed you the most.

I always thought,

How do you know

Before I even complete the words?

You sat with me by the reflecting waters of life.

As we looked within the reflection,

I saw there you were,

Holding on to me,

While I held on to you.

All the answers were there,

In the reflection.

My twin flame,

Eternally forever,

Is my

MIRROR IMAGE.

My Beloved Returns

MY BELOVED RETURNS

Wild blizzards ravishing upon the sea,

Made peace with the night

For they know this night is sanctified.

Thousands of nights,

The heavenly skies have poured in sorrow,

Rough storms have overpowered the Earth,

Yet tonight they all have befriended tranquility.

On this night, all are rejoicing.

The birds are singing.

The wind is playing his flutes.

Humans and animals have gone into their grottos.

Tonight, Mother Nature

Is dancing with joy.

Moonbows are appearing on top of the sea

As the moon is sparkling her glow

Upon the sea.

An enchanted phenomenal world

Has appeared tonight.

Tonight is proving to this world,

Love is timeless,

Love is bewitching,

Love is everlasting,

Love is true,

Truth is love.

Tonight,

MY BELOVED RETURNS.

MY DESTINATION

My love, life after life,

I entered the Ferris wheel,

In search for you.

I jumped on and off the Ferris wheel,

Without any fear,

Only for you.

I crossed oceans and lands,

Seeking simply, you.

Never did I fear death or life.

My only fear was,

What would I say when I do find you?

My determination is my complete faith,

For I know,

We are destined to meet,

For my journey will end up at your door.

For you, I was created,

As you were created for me.

The road,

The journey,

The hurdles,

The physical and emotional pain,

I never feared,

For with complete faith I knew,

Traveler I am

As you are

MY DESTINATION.

MY FIRST
AND LAST PRAYER

You are my first prayer of dawn

And first breath of the day.

Intoxicated within your embrace,

I can't break away

From under your spell.

The days dawn and the nights pass by,

Yet this mesmerizing love spell,

Never skips a beat.

The only beat that never stops

Is my heart,

For she races by in excitement

As she too is bound

Within your love potion.

If only I could bottle up my feelings,

And sprinkle upon this world,

The magical dust of love.

Awakened at dawn,

Would be people filled with love.

Never would anyone question,

Why you are but,

MY FIRST

AND LAST PRAYER.

MY NAME

At the first hour of dawn,

You call me your

Love.

When you hear my heartbeats, you say

Sweetheart.

I received your love letters

Marking my name as

Beloved.

Songs you have composed only for me,

Where you named me,

Darling.

Paintings you have fashioned after me,

Where you have said,

Gorgeous.

My love, you call my eyes,

Rivers of life.

Oh my darling,

You have said I am your

Bouquet of morning glories.

After strolling in the woods,

You have titled me your

Wildflowers.

Yet today I want you to

Call me only by your surname

For this life companion only has one wish,

May your name be

MY NAME.

My Struggles Became His Fight

MY STRUGGLES BECAME HIS FIGHT

Winter's storm appeared with a musical band.

Everything was dark,

With no echoes of any human,

Except nature displaying her fury in grand.

I walked in fear.

Lonely and wet,

I tried to escape nature's fury,

As someone held me from near.

Slouched and drenched in rain tumbling,

I tried to look up.

Slipping and sliding, I landed on you,

As you prevented me from falling.

Like the luminous light,

My twin flame appeared from the dim and forever now,

MY STRUGGLES

BECAME HIS FIGHT.

NEVER LET YOU GO

Forever love survives on.

Forever love is youthful.

You and I grow old,

Yet our love only grows in depth,

And remains young throughout time.

Eras shall pass,

And time shall bid her farewell.

Remember my love,

Even when you are old,

And I am frail,

Hold on to me for support.

For even then, I shall

Hold on to you for support.

For even then,

Keep me within your inner soul,

As I shall forever keep you in my soul.

For if ever,

My mind and body fail,

Even then forever,

I shall grasp on to our love and you,

For a promise made to you my love is,

I shall

NEVER LET YOU GO.

NOT LIFE
NOR DEATH

Born I am only to unite with and for you.

I open my eyes combing life after life,

Only for you.

I know we have rummaged for one another everlastingly.

Through the gates of my inner soul,

I have placed a call to you.

To reach the gates of your secret soul,

I have begun my voyage through life.

I know our eyes search for one another.

On top of the mountain,

Within the heated blazing sand dunes,

Upon the freezing snow-packed land,

And through the ocean whirlpool,

We wait for one another.

Faith keeps us strong.

Hope ignites like a candle,

Never giving up,

For we know we shall meet,

For the union shall be,

For we fear nothing,

NOT LIFE

NOR DEATH.

OCEAN OF LOVE

Life after life,

I sought you.

Within my inner eyes,

I found you

Searching and waiting for me.

My love,

Our eyes had become an ocean,

Where true love decants out from.

As tears emptied out of my eyes,

You held on to them.

Never did you allow the ocean of tears

To get lost

For you were asleep

Floating upon the ocean of tears.

It is then I opened my eyes,

And held on to your tears.

Our eyes had enunciated our love to one another,

Throughout eternity.

With eyes upon eyes,

You read my mind,

As I read yours.

In union,

We created the everlasting

OCEAN OF LOVE.

ONLY FOR YOU

Life awakened me with a gift,

When you became my life.

Lost, stranded, and hurt I was,

Until you awakened my inner soul.

Why was I born,

I had asked myself

As you stood there in front of me.

Everybody belongs somewhere,

What about me,

I kept on asking.

When I came to the end of my thread,

I found you.

Love filled within your eyes,

You held on to me.

Without saying anything,

You responded to my lifelong queries.

Simple yet complete remedies came,

From a lover to a beloved,

ONLY FOR YOU.

OWN WORLD

Love is life,

Generated through

The union of

Heaven and Earth.

I find comfort from the intense sun,

On a cold, snow-white morning,

From a cool ocean breeze blowing in peace,

And under gray skies pouring cool showers.

All of this is found within my framed canvas,

Where enchanted rainbows paint

A backdrop for true lovers in this home.

Here within this setting, I find

Eternal love protected under a cover,

Warm on a snow-covered day,

Cool within heated summer twilights.

No home is needed,

Nor any luxuries of the

Earth beneath or skies above,

For here I live with my

Twin flame.

Here we have created

A home,

A vicinity,

A realm,

With one another

For this is our

OWN WORLD.

Parted Myself From Me

PARTED MYSELF
FROM ME

Candle glowing in the wind,

Burns herself

To glow for her beloved.

The light glowing

Through the window

Has separated from the moon.

All the glowing sparkles

Romance within us.

We accept the light

And glow as lovebirds.

The radiance of the light

Shines upon us,

And teaches us to

Give for one another,

Give to one another,

Give,

And get back much more.

So, like the moon's gleam,

I became your luminosity.
To be only and truly yours, I
PARTED MYSELF
FROM ME.

SLEEPLESS
THROUGHOUT THE NIGHTS

Like a night owl,

You called upon my window.

I answered your call and realized,

This call has taken my mind, body, and soul.

I was by myself, lonesome in the dark,

Waiting for a flute player

To take me on a fairy-tale ride.

This enchanted call has now given me

Everything in life.

Yet this call has robbed my sleep.

For love, you call upon me,

As I call upon you.

In union,

We are both,

SLEEPLESS

THROUGHOUT THE NIGHTS.

SPELLBOUND AND INTOXICATED

Charmed forest burns like embers

As it feels our rising,

Our blending.

Enchanted love brew becomes a cascade,

In the enraptured

Land of twin flames.

The rivers become nectar

For all lovebirds.

The land becomes mystical,

Sheltering twin flames from all sinful eyes.

The fairy-tale dreamland

All true lovers search for,

Is not what my eyes pursue,

For this old soul,

This beloved of yours,

Only seeks you.

Within your embrace,

Within your chest,

Keep me safe throughout eternity,

For this lovebird is wildly in love

With you.

For you and only you,

I am,

SPELLBOUND AND

INTOXICATED.

Standing At The Riverbend

STANDING AT THE RIVERBEND

At the riverbend,

I wait for you.

Wandering life after life,

I have awakened only for you.

Attending to the sweet songs of hope

Kept my feet going.

All my tears spread upon Earth for you,

Have produced rivers, oceans, and lakes.

You shall see my reflection,

Upon the reflecting waters of life.

You shall hear my voice,

Within the rainforests of this Earth.

Within a star-filled night,

Wish upon a star, my love.

Like the phenomenal bridge of a rainbow,

We shall materialize to one another.

Our hands shall be tied in a knot,

Flowers shall blossom within love,

And the moon shall be glorified with harmony.

When we shall unite

With one another,

The Earth and Heaven shall sing,

Forever be mine,

As we shall perform for everyone,

Be mine,

STANDING AT THE RIVERBEND.

SUNSET SONGS

The hour of sunset has arrived

Above the world.

Yet tonight I am not afraid of the dark

For on this night,

I have you.

The sunset above the vast skies,

Is vision of our love.

A painter with his loving brush strokes,

Has framed upon the skies,

Our love story,

Which no human can view,

Not even the birds

For this is a sacred sanctuary

For two hearts.

All the birds have returned home.

Even morning glories have

Fallen asleep.

Only sleepless at this time

To witness this magical aura

Are we the lovers.

Deeply entranced within one another,

We keep this night,

This hour,

This twinkling alive,

Entwined within one another.

Within our eternal vows,

We recite the

SUNSET SONGS.

TEARS

Tears talk when I don't.

Anger diminishes

Into tears when I see you.

Words get lost within me,

As I try to voice them into air,

For I am evermore yours,

As I kept my promise.

My love, I only ask,

Remember your promises.

You call upon me after the heavens

Fill up the night skies,

With glimmering stars.

You hold on to me under the moonlit skies.

I search for you when all is dark.

I seek you when I am drenched,

Within the appalling stormy nights.

You appear over and over and hold on to me,

When I am about to fall.

Yet within the daylight hours,

When the sun inundates the Earth,

It is then, you and I are so far apart.

Today, I pray you and I are never apart,

Across time and space.

I pray,

Today, tomorrow, and throughout time,

You be mine,

As forever I am yours.

This signed sealed poem

From the heart is written with love.

Remember my love,

Forever eternally yours I am.

Promises made are

My oath for today and forever,

Eternally signed with my

TEARS.

TIME STANDS IMMOBILE

Time passes by yet love lives on.

For you, I am and

For me, my love, you are.

Never young nor old,

Our love is always in the present.

Our oath is never-ending.

Throughout time,

Throughout eternity,

I have crossed all borders.

I have taken all trials.

Nothing is unbearable.

Nothing is impossible.

For you, I have crossed even the doors beyond,

Known as death and ever after.

For me, you have awakened.

For me, you have risen

From the door of death.

For us, Heaven above and Earth beneath,

Have bestowed their blessings.

As our love has been accepted

By Heaven above and Earth beneath,

Forever now even

TIME STANDS

IMMOBILE.

True Nightingales

TRUE NIGHTINGALES

My beloved,

My everlasting love,

The night stars chaperoned me to you.

The dreamy musical tunes

Knocked upon my inner passion,

Awakening my weary, sleepy soul.

Your calls came

Through the voice of a nightingale.

I followed your nightly songs,

Without any fear.

Attracted only to you I was

For the stars guided me

To a flame sturdier than any bond.

Ever passionate flames

Awakened the night skies.

Nothing was visible,

But you and me.

The Earth, the skies, and the stars,

Witnessed a union,

Between you and me,
As your musical night calls united us,
TRUE NIGHTINGALES.

TWO BODIES
YET ONE SOUL

Through life and through death,

We have promised

To be in unification.

As nightingales singing through the dark skies,

Or as phoenixes rising from ashes,

You are mine

As I am only yours.

If I ever get lost,

May you guide me back,

For you are always my shadow.

If you find yourself in the dark,

Worry not my love,

For I will always glimmer

As a night star above you.

Unconnected as born on Earth we have become,

Yet my love for you

And your love for me

Keep us as twin flames

Throughout eternity,

For we have

TWO BODIES

YET ONE SOUL.

WITHIN MY DREAMS

Tonight, my love,

Let hope spread.

Let the full moon sparkle upon our window

For even she knows tonight you are here.

The stars upon the skies are twinkling

For they are seeking my attention.

They are all jealous

As I left them alone on this night

For tonight,

I don't need anyone to talk with.

On this night, I have you.

My love,

Thousands of years,

I have waited for you.

A sprinkle of miracle

Landed upon my window of hope,

As you appeared from this dust.

Are you real or is this another dream?

I pleaded with the night, the moon, and all the stars,

To never take away my dreams,

For I search only for you

WITHIN MY DREAMS.

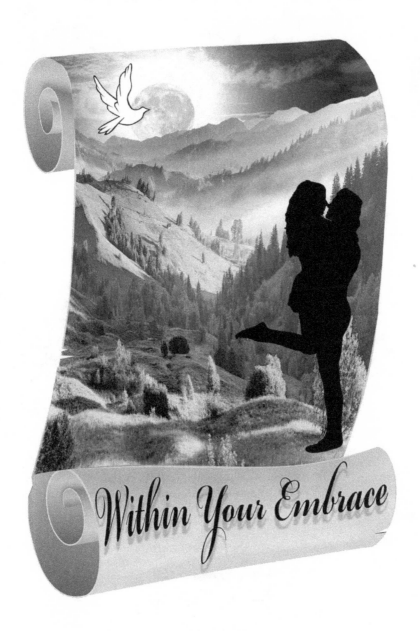

WITHIN YOUR EMBRACE

Hands in hands,

We began the journey.

Forever I was dazzled

By your eyes,

As your eyes said nothing

But just gazed back.

Promises were made

Without uttering any words.

You understood the silence,

As I only heard your heartbeats.

The sparkling stars

Glowed on our path.

The cool breeze

On a summer's night,

Was our confidant.

The northern mockingbird,

Hummed for us all

Throughout the night.

All of them knew,

As did Mother Earth,

On this night and forever,

I am

WITHIN YOUR EMBRACE.

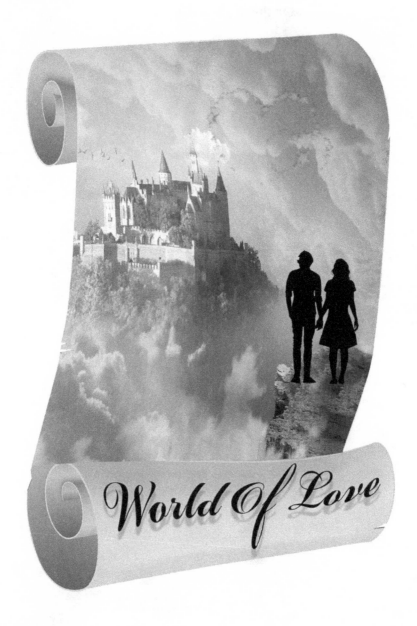

WORLD OF LOVE

You and I, is us,

And this is our love.

From this sanctified union,

We have created an alternative world

Where stars in the night skies

Create Cupid's bow and arrow,

And where flowers bloom as high as mountains tall.

Here you will always find me always,

As I have found you while I sought.

Never shall we be lost to one another,

As we are steered to each other,

Through our inner eyes of love.

Even in death,

Or in life,

We shall eternally

Be in union

In this heavenly place.

For this place,

We have created,

You and I, is us,

To all, this is known as,

WORLD OF LOVE.

WRITE YOUR NAME

Your heartbeats called upon my heart,

As I landed within your home.

Sweet musical songs kept on playing,

As I was led to a mystical room.

My eyes searched all around,

For I knew the room.

So familiar were the open windows.

Flying white curtains,

Also sang to me.

With amusement and amazement,

I walked into this room.

Never had I entered this Heaven,

Yet this was all known to me.

I asked you,

Where am I?

You showed me the walls,

Where I saw my name

Glittered like gold,

Written over the years

With so much love.

You asked me lovingly,

Would I next to my name,

WRITE YOUR NAME?

YOUR CALL IS
MY HEARTBEAT

Standing by the ocean,

I waited for your signs.

The waves started to talk with me,

And we even sang together.

I learned to swim in the cold freezing ocean,

For endurance was the food I lived on.

To quench my thirst,

I tried to take a drink from the salty ocean water.

My eyes found an ocean,

Yet none of it was drinkable.

Again, your thoughts pierced

Through my chest.

My salty tears have formed an ocean.

My inner agony longing for you is known as

The nightingale's tears through the nights.

Yet my love, you are not seen,

Nor can you be heard,

Nor can you be touched.

If only tears could make you drift

Toward me,

I would contentedly create ocean after ocean,

To at least once swim with you.

Yet as I became a dry sandy desert,

I saw your dedicated footprints.

I heard your fragranced songs.

I felt your tender touch

As you chanted,

YOUR CALL IS

MY HEARTBEAT.

YOUR EYES, MY TEARS

Heavenly rain poured upon Earth and ocean.

Earth finally kissed the ocean water.

My tears emptied nonstop,

Yet my pain never touched anyone.

Eternity passed by,

Yet my eyes never hurt from all the pouring tears.

I desired for my twin flame,

Life after life.

I crossed ocean after ocean,

As I found myself awakened in foreign lands

And different times.

Yet my eyes never hurt,

Even though my soul's moaning sounds,

Heartened all even in Heaven above.

I sought my beloved upon Earth and Heaven,

As I watched him pursuing me.

His pain-filled cries reached my soul,

As I realized my pain-filled cries,

Had reached his.

I asked him endlessly,

As I have spilled my tears,

Hoping he would find me,

In the love's reflecting weeping lakes.

I asked him but why did I not feel the tears?

He answered all my questions,

For he said,

YOUR EYES, MY TEARS.

YOUR GIFT

The pleasant sun has gifted the Earth,

Glorious breakthrough at dawn.

The glittering moon has gifted this Earth

With her lantern of guidance

For the dark nights.

Mother Earth has gifted this Earth,

Her children.

Sweet songs are gifts

From a singer to her fans.

An artist gifts her canvas and paintings

As a forever gem to the world.

Yet for my darling,

My blessed twin flame,

The one I kept hidden within my chest,

For thousands of years,

I only have a simple present.

This treasure you can keep

Throughout time.

You can never misplace this,

Or return this,

For this gift will be yours

Throughout this life

And thereafter.

To you, I give

My eternal love,

As

YOUR GIFT.

YOUR SHADOW

The moon shining upon the river of life,

Is only a reflection.

I want to immerge myself within you,

Not just when seen in a reflection,

But deeply entwined within your embrace,

Immensely in love with one another,

Where if one exists,

Then the other one exists too.

Where you are, I am.

Where you are lost, I am not found.

When I think,

It is you who voices the thought.

When I feel hurt,

I find tears falling from your eyes.

On a cold winter night,

You become my warm cozy fire.

You lay on top of me,

As you protect me

From pouring sweet raindrops.

Now, I want to be your lover.

I want to be your life.

I want to be yours eternally,

So, I have become forever

YOUR SHADOW.

CONCLUSION

Twin flames and the concept of twin flames have survived time. Eyewitnesses to this theory have taken birth from the beginning of time and we shall continue to have evermore eyewitnesses till time's end. Separated are all twin flames to become an individual, yet they unite to be complete. It is true they can survive as an individual but in union, they are complete.

This need, this longing of the soul, to find the other half is everlasting. It is a thirst that is never fulfilled until you have completely united with your other half. This need and desire is so grand, nothing but one's twin flame can satisfy this thirst.

As I stood next to the North Sea, I knew all the salty water in front of my eyes could not content my thirst. Only a glass of fresh and clean mountain spring water could please my physical thirst. This world is full of men and women, yet only one's twin flame can complete the yearning and desires of the other half.

Through this book for all of you, I have written love poems. These poems are for all the twin flames who have searched for one another. Some of you have found one another and some of you are still searching.

My message in conclusion would be to never give up. Your search is your love story and the time apart is your memories to share. You will find your other half only if you pursue him or her.

In the meantime, I would want you to be inspired by my love poems written with complete love for my twin flame. These poems will be your after sunset hour inspiration to dream a little. They will be your hope from sunrise to sunset. During the days when your best friend, tears, gives you a visit, do narrate them again.

This book is my gift for all the lost and stranded lovers. Through a poem, I found my desires and yearnings make peace. Like a loaf of fresh baked bread, I have within this book left something for all the lovebirds to perform and share with one another.

This is my gift for your wedding. You will narrate these everlasting poems at your weddings as you unite forever with your twin flame. These timeless treasured poems will take a blessed turn as you find this book as your forever book to keep and pass on to your future generation.

May my poetry be the thirst quencher for all true love and lovers. May love take birth from true lovers amongst all of you. Remember to protect this blessed bond sacredly beneath the wings of my sweet poems written for you. Do recite them, sing them, and quench your enchanted thirst for love and its pure essence of everlasting spells today and throughout time.

This book of poetry, my sweet everlasting songs, is my personal gift to all twin flames of today and forever. Treasure this book today and forever tomorrow. I call this book *Love Letters: The Timeless Treasure.*

ABOUT THE AUTHOR

Ann Marie Ruby is an international number-one bestselling author. She has been a spiritual friend through her books. The bond between her readers and herself has been created through her books. You have all respected her privacy as she wanted to remain private, never questioned about her pictures, yet gave her your complete love without judging.

Some of you, the readers, had gone to the point where you too completely understood her request to remain private. The blessed readers around the globe have made Ann Marie's books bestsellers internationally. She has become from your love, an international number-one bestselling author.

This love that you poured to an unknown author had awakened her inner self and she wanted to give you her gift and reveal her face to this world. So, on the publication of her twelfth book, she revealed herself and became the known face giving you her blessings throughout time. All of you can see Ann Marie on her website and her social media pages.

If this world would have allowed, she would have distributed all of her books to you with her own hands as a gift and a message from a friend. She has taken pen to paper to spread peace throughout this Earth. Her sacred soul has found peace within herself as she says, "May I through my words bring peace and solace within your soul."

As many of you know, Ann Marie is also a dream psychic and a humanitarian. As a dream psychic, she has correctly predicted personal and global events. Some of these events have come true in front of us in the year 2020. She has also seen events from the past. You can read more about her journey as a dream psychic in *Spiritual Lighthouse: The Dream Diaries Of Ann Marie Ruby* which many readers have said is "the best spiritual book" they have read. As a humanitarian, she has taken pen to paper to end hate crimes within *The World Hate Crisis: Through The Eyes Of A Dream Psychic.*

To unite all race, color, and religion, following her dreams, Ann Marie has written two religiously unaffiliated prayer books, *Spiritual Songs: Letters From My Chest* and *Spiritual Songs II: Blessings From A Sacred Soul*, which people of all faiths can recite.

Ann Marie's writing style is known for making readers feel as though they have made a friend. She has written four books of original inspirational quotations which have also been compiled in one book, *Spiritual Ark: The Enchanted Journey Of Timeless Quotations.*

154

As a leading voice in the spiritual space, Ann Marie frequently discusses spiritual topics. As a spiritual person, she believes in soul families, reincarnation, and dreams. For this reason, she answers the unanswered questions of life surrounding birth, death, reincarnation, soulmates and twin flames, dreams, miracles, and end of time within her book *Eternal Truth: The Tunnel Of Light*. Readers have referred to this book as one of the must-read and most thought-provoking books.

The Netherlands has been a topic in various books by Ann Marie. As a dream psychic, she constantly has had dreams about this country before ever having any plan to visit the country or any previous knowledge of the contents seen within her dreams. Ann Marie's love and dreams of the Netherlands brought her to write *The Netherlands: Land Of My Dreams* which became an overnight number-one bestseller and topped international bestselling lists.

To capture not just the country but her past inhabitants, Ann Marie brought for this country, *Everblooming: Through The Twelve Provinces Of The Netherlands*, a keepsake for all generations to come. This book also became an overnight number-one bestseller and topped international bestselling lists. Readers have called this book "the best book ever." They have asked for this book to be included in schools for all to read and cherish.

Love Letters: The Timeless Treasure is Ann Marie's thirteenth book. Within this book, Ann Marie has gifted her readers fifty of her soul-touching love poems. She calls these poems, love letters. These are individual stories, individual love letters to a beloved, from a lover. In a poetic way, she writes to her twin flame. These poems are her gifts to all loving souls, all twin flames throughout time. All poems have an individual illustration retelling the stories, which Ann Marie designed herself.

You have her name and know she will always be there for anyone who seeks her. Ann Marie's home is Washington State, USA, yet she travels all around the world to find you, the human with humanity.

Aside from her books, she loves writing blog posts and articles openly on her website. She has also interviewed award-winning individuals and organizations. Through the journey of her blog, she is available to all throughout this world. Come journey together and spread positivity, as she takes you on a positive journey through her website alongside her books. Remember you too can be a part of her journey.

For more information about Ann Marie Ruby, any one of her books, or to read her blog posts and articles, subscribe to her website, www.annmarieruby.com.

Follow Ann Marie Ruby on social media:

Twitter: @AnnahMariahRuby
Facebook: @TheAnnMarieRuby
Instagram: @Ann_Marie_Ruby
Pinterest: @TheAnnMarieRuby

BOOKS BY THE AUTHOR

INSPIRATIONAL QUOTATIONS:

I have published four books of original inspirational quotations:

Spiritual Travelers:
Life's Journey From The Past
To The Present
For The Future

Spiritual
Messages:
From A Bottle

Spiritual Journey:
Life's Eternal Blessings

Spiritual
Inspirations:
Sacred Words
Of Wisdom

For all of you whom have requested my complete inspirational quotations, I have my complete ark of inspiration, I but call:

Spiritual Ark:
The Enchanted Journey Of Timeless
Quotations

THE SPIRITUAL SONGS COLLECTION:

When there was no hope, I found hope within these sacred words of prayers, I but call songs. Within this book, I have for you, 100 very sacred prayers:

Spiritual Songs:
Letters From My Chest

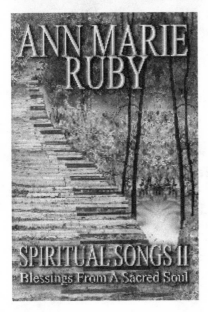

Prayers are but the sacred doors to an individual's enlightenment. This book has 123 prayers for all humans with humanity:

Spiritual Songs II:
Blessings From A Sacred
Soul

SPIRITUAL COLLECTION:

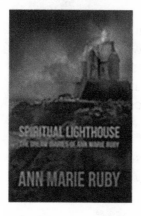

Do you believe in dreams? For within each individual dream, there is a hidden message and a miracle interlinked. Learn the spiritual, scientific, religious, and philosophical aspects of dreams. Walk with me as you travel through forty nights, through the pages of my book:

Spiritual Lighthouse:
The Dream Diaries Of Ann Marie Ruby

Humans have walked into an age where humanity now is being questioned as hate crimes have reached a catastrophic amount. Let us in union stop this crisis. Pick up my book and see if you too could join me in this fight:

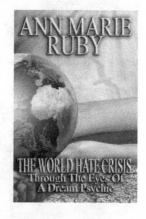

The World Hate Crisis:
Through The Eyes Of A Dream Psychic

Travel with me through the doors of birth, death, reincarnation, true soulmates, dreams, miracles, end of time, and the:

Eternal Truth:
The Tunnel Of Light

160

THE NETHERLANDS:

Oh the sacred travelers, be like the mystical river and journey through this blessed land through my book. Be the flying bird of wisdom and learn about a land I call, Heaven on Earth. For you the traveler, this is:

The Netherlands:
Land Of My Dreams

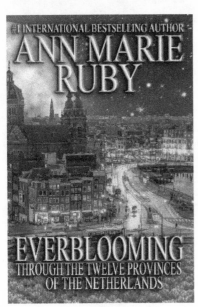

Original poetry and hand-picked tales are bound together in this keepsake book. Come travel with me as I take you through the lives of the Dutch past. I call them:

Everblooming:
Through The Twelve
Provinces Of The
Netherlands

161

POETRY:

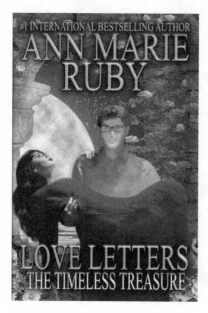

Fifty original timeless treasured love poems are presented with individual illustrations describing each poem. I call this treasured book of poetry:

Love Letters:
The Timeless Treasure

CPSIA information can be obtained
at www.ICGtesting.com
Printed in the USA
LVHW112225191122
733619LV00022B/202